D0791896

The Vulture

The Vulture

By Susan Schafer

DILLON PRESS
New York

Maxwell Macmillan Canada
Toronto

Maxwell Macmillan International
New York   Oxford   Singapore   Sydney

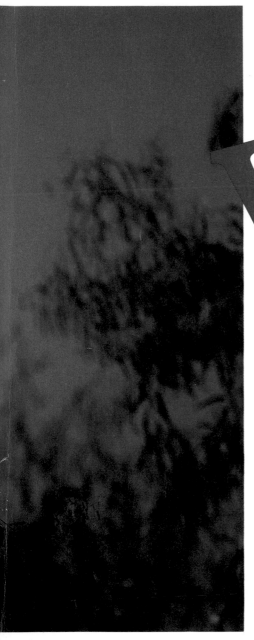

Acknowledgments

My sincerest gratitude to Bill Toone, curator of birds at the San Diego Wild Animal Park, for his thorough review of the manuscript; to my editor and friend, Joyce Stanton, for her perceptive work and hardy support; to the staff of the Charles Paddock Zoo; to Dave Rimlinger and Wayne Schulenberg at the San Diego Zoo; and to my biggest fan, my husband, Paul Severtson.

Photo Credits

Photographs courtesy of Susan Schafer

Drawing on page 23 by Susan Schafer

Book design by Carol Matsuyama

Library of Congress Cataloging-in-Publication Data

Schafer, Susan.
      The vulture / by Susan Schafer. — 1st ed.
         p. cm. — (Remarkable animals)
      Includes bibliographical references (p.   ) and index.
      ISBN 0-87518-604-1
      1. Turkey vulture—Juvenile literature. [1. Turkey vulture. 2. Vultures.] I.
   Title. II. Series: Remarkable animal series.
   QL696.F33S35 1994
   598.9' 12—dc20   93-44534

Describes the physical characteristics, habits, and life cycle of the turkey vulture, an important scavenger, as well as its related species in the Americas.

Dillon Press   Maxwell Macmillan Canada, Inc.
Macmillan Publishing Company   1200 Eglinton Avenue East
866 Third Avenue   Suite 200
New York, NY 10022   Don Mills, Ontario M3C 3N1

Macmillan Publishing Company is part of the Maxwell Communication Group of Companies.

First edition

Printed in the United States of America

10 9 8 7 6 5 4 3 2 1

0-382-24725-6 (pbk.)

Contents

Facts about the Turkey Vulture

Scientific Name: *Cathartes aura*

Description:

Length—2.2 to 2.7 feet (0.66 to 0.83 meter); wingspan 5.7 to 6 feet (1.7 to 1.8 meters)

Weight—Less than 3 pounds (1.4 kilograms)

Physical Features—Bare head and neck, head small compared with hawk's and eagle's; strong beak; weak feet; long, broad wings

Color—Black body; undersides of wings are black on the front half and milky gray on the back half; adults have a red head and neck; young have an ash gray head and neck; nestlings are covered with soft, off-white down

Distinctive Habits: Most often seen soaring in wide circles high in the sky, perched on trees or posts, or feeding on carrion on the ground; roosts at night in tall trees or on rocky cliffs, often in large groups

Food: Primarily carrion

Reproductive Cycle: Females normally lay two creamy white eggs, usually mottled with brown, in the spring; no nest—eggs are laid on the ground in the hollows of rocks, cliffs, and logs; eggs hatch in about 38 to 41 days; both parents care for the eggs and the young; young take their first flight about two to three months after hatching

Life Span: Long-lived, more than 24 years

Range: Reaches from southern Canada, throughout the United

States, south through Mexico and Central America, to the lower tip of South America

Habitat: The open sky over all types of terrain except for dense forests

Range of the Turkey Vulture

Chapter 1

Nature's Garbage Disposals

A dust devil rises in the wind from the sun-baked ground and spins off into the distance like a dancer twirling to music. For a moment the wind dies, and everything is still. Then the wind kicks up again, and a large shadow appears on the open plain and skates across the ground toward a small group of big, glistening black birds.

Suddenly the shadow's owner drops from the sky, beating the air with its long wings as it touches down. Joining the other birds at the body of a dead animal, it reaches to get at the best morsels. Before long, not much will remain of the **carcass*** but bones and flaps of hairy hide. Nature's garbage disposals, the turkey vultures, are hard at work

*Words in **bold type** are explained in the glossary at the end of this book.

feeding themselves—and, in the process, keeping the environment clean.

Without the many kinds of vultures in the world, the bodies of dead animals would rot on the ground, smelling and attracting flies that spread disease. By feeding on carcasses, vultures tidy up the scraps on nature's platter. Then, like a cleansing rinse, the sun shines down and disinfects the ground.

Tools of the Trade

Like other kinds of vultures, the turkey vulture has a bare head, a long, featherless neck, and a hooked beak—**adaptations** that allow it to survive on its diet of dead animals. The bird's bare neck and head help keep it clean as it probes around the insides of a messy carcass. Feathers would only get in the way.

Its hooked beak also performs a specialized job. Just as surgeons use different instruments for different jobs, the type of beak a bird has depends

A turkey vulture tears flesh with its strong beak.

on what it eats. Birds that feed on seeds have stout beaks for crushing hard shells. Those that eat nectar have slender beaks for poking into flowers. The hooked beak of the turkey vulture is made for tearing meat. Along with the naked head and neck, it is one of the tools of this remarkable animal's trade.

Sharp Eyes, Keen Nose

Perched on the ground away from the bustle of the feeding crowd, a contented turkey vulture rests

Stretching its wings wide, a turkey vulture warms up in the sun.

with its wings stretched out to its sides, sunning itself and digesting its food. Behind it, a vast plain of scorched yellow grasses sweeps away into the distance. The hours the bird spent high in the sky patrolling for food have paid off.

For many years, scientists have argued whether the turkey vulture relies more on its sharp eyes to spot its **prey** from the sky or on its keen nose to locate it by smell. Like other **birds of prey**, it has excellent eyesight, but it also has the largest **olfactory system** of all birds.

While the argument continues, some studies show that smell alone would not enable the turkey vulture to detect the stench of rotting food from high altitudes. This is because odors vanish quickly in moving air. Most likely, both sight and smell are important senses for finding food, depending on the situation.

Weak Feet

A circling hawk drops suddenly from the sky, streaking toward a rustling movement in the grass far below. In the blink of an eye, like a broad jumper stretching out his or her legs to land, the hawk reaches out and plucks its prey from the ground with its strong, sharp claws.

The hawk, like all birds that attack and kill their prey, must be quick or its meal will escape. The prey of the turkey vulture, however, isn't going anywhere. The vulture needs only to find a meal,

13

land nearby, and casually walk up to the table. Its feet are weak compared with the hawk's and have short, flat claws rather than long, curved ones. The vulture's feet are adapted for walking, for perching, and for holding down a carcass while feeding.

Tough Tendons

When night falls, the turkey vulture retreats to the top of a tall tree or rocky cliff, grasping its night-time perch with its toes. But how does it keep from falling off its perch when it sleeps? As in all birds, the grip of its toes is tightened by tough, cordlike **tendons** that run along the bones of its feet. When a bird squats down into a resting position, the tendons in its feet automatically pull its toes inward, tightening its grip around the perch. The bird may be relaxed in sleep, but its feet are not.

Imagine attaching a string to each of your fingers and then joining those five strings through your wrist to a single string running up your arm. If you pulled on your arm string, your fingers

A turkey vulture's flat feet are well adapted for walking.

would close tightly in the palm of your hand, just as a bird's toes close around a perch. To loosen its grip, a bird must raise itself up off its feet to release the tendons in its toes.

Master of the Winds

A turkey vulture circles in the sky, its wings held steady in a V position, its body tipping slightly from side to side as it peers down on the country-side far below it. Nearly motionless on the wind, it might not beat its wings for hours. Then in an

Gripping a branch with the strong tendons in its toes, a turkey vulture settles in for the night.

instant it might glide downward at 60 miles (97 kilometers) an hour, faster than the speed limit for cars on most highways.

While most birds achieve flight by flapping their wings and propelling themselves forward, the turkey vulture spends most of its time soaring and gliding on the winds. By stretching its wings wide, the bird lifts itself up into the sky on warm, rising currents of air. By flexing, or bending, its wings, it glides smoothly back down again. Soaring up and gliding down throughout the day, the vulture rides the roller coaster of the winds.

Rising with the Heat

Early in the morning, the cool night air warms with the rising sun. The turkey vulture, perched atop the twisted branch of an old, dead tree, waits for its time to fly. The longer it takes for the day to warm up, the longer the vulture will have to wait before it begins its search for food.

When the time is right, rising columns of warm air, called thermals, lift the turkey vulture into the sky like the heat blown into a hot air balloon. To stay within a thermal, the vulture soars in large circles, sometimes as wide as a football field from sideline to sideline.

A Perfect Landing

Using its tail to steer, like a captain turning the rudder of a ship, the turkey vulture changes directions

A turkey vulture prepares to fly.

by tilting its tail to one side or the other. To slow down, it lowers and spreads out the feathers of its tail to create drag. By throwing its body upright at the same time and beating its wings like a swimmer doing the backstroke, it slows itself down further for landing. At the last moment, the turkey vulture stretches its wings out to the side for balance and absorbs the shock of the landing with its springy legs.

By feeding on dead animals, the vulture helps keep the earth clean.

Back on the ground, the vulture returns to its business as nature's garbage disposal, cleaning up the earth and feasting contentedly on the remains of carcasses that few other animals would touch.

Chapter 2

The Giants of Flight

Around the world, about 20 **species**, or kinds, of vultures fly above the desert, plains, and forests. Seven of these, including the turkey vulture, make their home in North, Central, and South America. The turkey vulture is the one people most often see in the Americas, and its relatives are among the largest birds alive today. Its ancestors, though, were the largest birds ever to have lived.

A vulture ancestor that thrived around 70 million years ago is the largest flying bird on record. Its **fossil** was discovered at the La Brea tar pits in California, where it had been preserved. With its wings spread wide, *Teratornis incredibilis*, the "incredible revolving monster," measured a colos-

For more than 70 million years, vultures have looked down on the earth from their soaring positions high in the sky.

sal 18 feet (5.5 meters) from wing tip to wing tip.

The largest vulture alive today, the Andean condor of South America, has a wingspan that regularly reaches more than 10 feet (3 meters).

Feathered Reptiles

Birds **evolved** from reptilian ancestors called **thecodonts**, who roamed the earth about 200 million years ago, long before the vulture's ancestors came along. Small and scaly, they ran on their hind legs and climbed trees. Some jumped from the trees and glided through the air.

The earliest bird, *Archaeopteryx,* was basically a lizard, except that it had feathers. About the size of a crow, it lived around 150 million years ago. Scientists have carefully studied the bird's fossil remains. Its skeleton suggests it was a weak flier, and its feathers suggest that it was not cold-blooded like its reptilian ancestors, but warm-blooded like the birds of today. Scientists group all birds in a **class** of their own, called Aves, because they share a common feature: They are the only **verte-brates** that have feathers.

The Fabulous Feather

The feather is one of the lightest, but at the same time one of the strongest, structures to grow out of the skin of an animal. The hairs and nails of other animals are simple by comparison. A single feather is divided into more than a million bristlelike parts. These all grow out from a central support and lock together through a series of hooks to form a strong, flat surface.

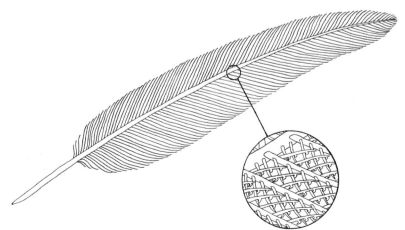

A typical feather with a close-up view

23

A vulture tips its head forward to preen. Preening keeps its feathers in good shape for flying.

To keep their feathers in top working condition, birds spend several hours every day **preening**. By pulling disorderly feathers through their beaks, they rearrange them into their proper order. Together, all the feathers on a bird work to insulate it from the cold, waterproof it against the rain, and help it to fly.

24

Eagle or Stork?

Until recently, scientists have **classified** all of the world's vultures in the order, or large group, of birds called Falconiformes. Known as diurnal birds of prey, which means they hunt during the day rather than at night, this group also includes the eagle, hawk, falcon, osprey, and secretary bird. They all have powerful wings, hooked beaks, and the long-range vision of a person using binoculars. While vultures feed on carrion, or dead animals, other falconiformes, with their curved, grasping feet, catch live animals.

Today, many scientists believe that the American vultures, like the turkey vulture, should be classified in a different order, called Ciconii-formes. This is a group of wading birds that includes the storks and flamingos. The American vultures may look and act like other vultures, with their colored bald heads and fondness for carrion, but their skulls, beaks, and feet are more like those of storks.

A Nose with a View

The **perforated** beaks and flat feet of the storks and American vultures distinguish them from the other birds of prey. As if pierced through by a power drill, the nostrils atop their beaks do not have a soft wall dividing them. Like looking through a keyhole into a room, you could peek through the nostrils of a turkey vulture and admire the countryside beyond.

Whether classified with the hawks or moved to the storks, American vultures belong to a family, or smaller group, called the Cathartidae. In North America, the family includes three species: the turkey vulture, the black vulture, and the California condor. In Central and South America, it includes four species: two kinds of yellow-headed vultures, the king vulture, and the Andean condor.

Vultures of the North

The turkey vulture has the widest range of the seven species, reaching from Canada to the southern

You can look straight through the nostrils of a turkey vulture and see the background beyond.

tip of South America. Adults measure about 2.5 feet long (0.8 meter) and have wingspans of about 6 feet (1.8 meters). Although about the size of an eagle, the turkey vulture weighs less than 3 pounds (1.4 kilograms).

The turkey vulture's smaller cousin, the black vulture, is only about 2 feet long (0.6 meter), with a wingspan of about 5 feet (1.5 meters). It lives

27

primarily in the southern half of the United States, but also ranges through Central and South America. As the name implies, it has a black head.

California's giant vulture, the California condor, measures up to 4.6 feet in length (1.4 meters). Its wingspan is normally about 9 feet (2.7 meters), although it sometimes reaches 11 feet (3.4 meters). If you and a friend joined hands and stretched as wide as you could without letting go, you would be about the same width as a soaring condor. The California condor, one of North America's rarest birds, has smooth, yellow-red skin on its head and neck.

Vultures of the South

The two yellow-headed vultures of the **tropical** regions of southern Mexico and northern South America look almost exactly like the turkey vulture. The main difference, as you may have guessed, is that they have a yellowish head.

Riding the skies above the rain forests and

Less than half the size of the giant Andean condor, the black vulture is the smallest American vulture.

plains of southern Mexico through South America is the king vulture. The most colorful of the vultures, its bare red, blue, and black head and neck are decorated with bright orange warts and bulging red wattles.

The Andean condor lives high in the Andes, a mountain chain that runs along the entire continent of South America from north to south. Its bare head and neck are dark gray and wrinkled like some alien creature, and its forehead is crowned with a thick, swollen wattle like an inflated comb atop a giant rooster.

What's in a Name?

The turkey vulture's scientific name is *Carthartes aura*. It comes from the Latin words *catharticus*, meaning cleansing, and *aura*, meaning the air or a breeze.

The scientific name is a good description of the bird's behavior: Arriving and leaving upon the breeze, it diligently cleans the earth. Its common name—the turkey vulture—is not quite so accurate. While the turkey vulture has a red head and large body, its resemblance to a turkey goes no further.

The turkey vulture, like many animals, has several common names. Some people call it a buzzard, but true buzzards are actually hawks that live in Europe. When European settlers came to America, they mistook the vultures for their native buzzards. Because the turkey vulture loves carrion

The turkey vulture gets its name from its naked red head and big, black body.

and is black, it is sometimes called the "carrion crow." In Mexico it is sometimes called *gallinazo*, a word that, in Spanish, basically means "big, ugly chicken."

One name or many, the turkey vulture, like its giant ancestors and powerful relatives, continues to rule the skies.

Chapter 3

At Home in the Sky

Tracing circle after circle on the backdrop of the sky, turkey vultures patrol many different **habitats** but prefer wide, open spaces like those found on the North American prairies. They take advantage of pastures and farmlands where people have created open areas and are often seen at garbage dumps near towns.

A Fair Share for All

In its constant search for food, the turkey vulture soars for hours, sometimes rising to 10,000 feet to scan the countryside, but also to watch for distant vultures that might give a clue to the location of a meal. If one turkey vulture suddenly drops from

Spreading its wings and floating on the winds, a vulture is as much at home in the skies as a cloud.

When a turkey vulture discovers the body of an animal hit by a car, it will soon be joined by other vultures.

the sky and makes a beeline for the ground, other vultures that see it will head for the same spot.

Many vultures may gather from miles around to share in a feast. Does that seem unfair to the one that finds the food? It all works out in the end, because the vulture that discovers a meal today will share another vulture's food tomorrow.

34

Taking the Plunge at Mealtime

A large turkey vulture, its head wrinkled like a crumpled piece of red paper, casually approaches a carcass and calmly plucks out the animal's eyes. Plunging its beak into the stomach and intestines, the turkey vulture stuffs itself with as much food as possible. It might not find another meal for days.

A **connoisseur** of the disgusting, the vulture will eat any dead animal, whether it be as large as a beached whale or as small as a guppy. It also relishes any kind of waste, including animal excrement, sewer debris, discards from slaughterhouses, and moldy fruits and vegetables from garbage dumps.

Home for the Night

Above the hills beyond a grove of tall trees, several tiny specks of black appear upon the horizon. Slowly but steadily, the spots grow in the sky. The first wave of turkey vultures is approaching its **roost** for the night. At first, only a few land in the

The vulture's naked head helps to keep the bird clean when plunging into a carcass to feed.

tops of the trees, but soon a hundred or more may arrive.

Just as most people go about their business each day, returning home each night, vultures fly for miles to return to the same roosts each night. Sometimes a great many vultures share one roost. One of the largest vulture roosts ever reported in North America contained more than 1,000 birds.

Turkey vultures prefer the highest vantage

Vultures prefer roosts high above the ground, where they feel safe and have room to take off easily.

When the turkey vulture's wings are fully stretched, they can reach six feet.

points possible. They roost on high cliffs and tall trees or cacti. From their lofty positions, they are safe from **predators** like the coyote or wolf and have plenty of room to take off if they want to fly.

Sunbathers with Wings

A golden sun rises over a distant mountain, and a group of turkey vultures takes its first peek of the day. High in their roost, the birds spread their wings, sunbathing to recover from the cool of the night. By exposing as much of their bodies as possible, they warm up more quickly. If the night has been damp or rainy, spreading their wings helps the birds dry out as well.

Turkey vultures tolerate cool nights throughout their range, but those that live in or near Canada avoid the freezing winters. In the fall, they **migrate** south to warmer habitats in the United States, Mexico, and Central and South America, where they bask in the tropical sun like vacationing tourists.

Wherever they fly, from day to day or from season to season, turkey vultures always feel at home in the open skies.

Chapter 4

Silent Suitors

Above the green grasses of an oak-studded hill, an adult male turkey vulture circles a gliding female, hoping to catch her attention. It is spring in North America and time for the male to find a mate. The female, however, does not seem to notice him.

Suddenly, the male wheels around in the sky and dives toward the female, like a trick pilot impressing a crowd of spectators with his acrobatics. The female glides down the wind, and the male follows, circling, swooping, and wheeling around her.

Eventually the female, perhaps a little interested, lands in an open field and the male joins her.

During the breeding season, the wrinkled head of the male turkey vulture blushes a brilliant red.

Now is his chance to impress her. Parading in a circle like a clumsy, strutting rooster, the bird lifts his chest and raises his bent wings out to the side. Then, dropping his wings and shuffling forward upon his pinkish feet, he leans down and ducks his crinkled head, as if bowing politely to the female. Glimmering in the sunlight, the red skin of his head and neck is especially bright during the **breeding** season.

If the female accepts the male, they will mate and stay together for the rest of the breeding season. During this time, they will not return to their regular roost.

A Room with a View

Once they have paired up, the turkey vultures head for the high country to find a place to nest. They may choose a rocky, narrow crevice near the top of a sheer cliff, or a cave beneath a pile of gigantic boulders high on a hill.

While some nest in the cavity of an old stump

or in a hollow log or tree, most prefer a commanding view of the land around them. The more remote the nest, the more difficult it is for a predator to reach the vultures' helpless young.

Whatever site they choose, vultures don't actually build a nest. They simply lay their eggs on the ground on top of whatever dirt, stones, gravel, or leaf litter may be there.

A Clutch of Eggs

The total number of eggs that a female bird lays in a nest is called a clutch. The size of a clutch depends on the species and varies from one egg—the California condor's—to nearly forty—the bobwhite quail's. The female turkey vulture normally lays two eggs, but occasionally lays one or three. The eggs are about 3 inches (7.1 centimeters) long and 2 inches (4.8 centimeters) wide, about as large as jumbo-sized chicken eggs. Creamy white in color, they are speckled and splotched with brown, as if a messy candymaker had flecked

A mottled turkey vulture egg sits on the ground of a nest chamber.

chocolate syrup on them.

Usually, the turkey vulture lays only one clutch in a season. But if its eggs or young are destroyed, it may lay again.

Shared Duties

Deep within a rock crevice, a vulture sits on its eggs. Outside, its mate circles cautiously, choosing a time to enter the nest free from the watchful eye of a possible predator. Like most birds, turkey vultures are monogamous, which means that one male will stay with the same female throughout the breeding season.

Working together, the male and female **incubate**, or warm, the eggs, sometimes leaving the nest together to hunt for food, sometimes taking turns. Tirelessly, they keep their vigil, and in a little over a month—about thirty-eight to forty-one days—they receive their reward.

Breaking Free

A small crack appears on the surface of one of the mottled eggs. Soon another crack appears, and then a small chip of eggshell falls away. Inside the egg, a tiny vulture wiggles and squirms, using its egg tooth, a sharp, rough projection at the end of its bill, to scratch away at the wall of its prison.

Many hours pass. Occasionally, the tired little bird rests before resuming its work. Gradually, a

An adult turkey vulture, returning from feeding, cautiously approaches its nest deep within a boulder pit.

piece at a time, the eggshell weakens and breaks. Finally, the **hatchling** is free, its wrinkled, pink body damp with moisture. Its egg tooth, no longer needed, will soon fall off. Nearby, a small crack appears on the surface of the second egg.

For the first week after hatching, the parents brood the young constantly, never leaving them alone. Then they leave for longer and longer periods of time to search for food. Returning to the

46

nest, they feed the chicks by bringing up recently swallowed food. Thrusting its bill into its parent's mouth, looking as if it might disappear down the throat at any minute, a chick feeds greedily. Its plump **sibling**, already full and satisfied, sits with its head drooped forward, ready to sleep.

A New Generation of Disposals

Turkey vultures grow more slowly than other birds of prey. For two to three months, the chicks remain in the nest. By the time they are ready to take their first flight, they are close to adult size and have nearly all their feathers. Only a few soft tufts of white **down** stick out here and there from the black feathers.

Before venturing on their first flight, the young birds spend several days trying their wings. Climbing up onto a rock, they stretch their wings wide and flap them awkwardly against the air. At first they flap only a few times before resting. As they rest, they hop or walk about the rocks, picking

A young turkey vulture ventures from its nest to practice flapping its wings. Someday its black head will turn red.

48

up twigs with their beaks and plucking at fallen leaves, perhaps practicing for their first nibbles on a meal of carrion. Each day they leave the nest for short periods to repeat their exercises. With time, their muscles develop and they flap their wings more boldly, sometimes lifting themselves up slightly into the air.

Then, early one morning, the wind rises briskly from the valley and up past the nest. One of the young birds moves close to the edge of the rocks. Lifting its wings and flapping, it suddenly hops into the sky and is carried away across the valley on the breeze. The young bird, ready to clean up Mother Earth, has taken its place among a new generation of turkey vultures.

Chapter 5

Saved Before the Nick of Time

Many animals in the world today are **endangered**. Some, like the California condor, have been saved in the nick of time—just before the last of the birds died out. With time and attention, they have been helped to repopulate their natural habitats.

Perhaps the day has come, however, for people to save wildlife before the nick of time, long before their numbers become so small that the animals might be lost forever.

Blight or Benefit?

The turkey vulture is not yet an endangered species, although its numbers have declined over much of its range. As with so many animals in the

The turkey vulture is one of many animals in the world that need protection before they become endangered.

world today, human beings have been its worst enemy.

For many years, people feared that the vulture carried livestock diseases, such as anthrax and hog cholera, because the birds fed on animals that had died from these diseases. By the time it was proved otherwise, thousands of vultures had been shot and killed.

Many more turkey vultures died from eating poisoned carcasses that were put out by ranchers to kill coyotes. Much of the vulture's nesting habitat was also destroyed by farming and urban development. Fewer and fewer places were available for it to raise its young.

Today most people recognize that turkey vultures are a benefit to the environment. They clear away dead and decaying animals and help to prevent the spread of disease. A valued **scavenger**, the turkey vulture is now protected by law in the United States along with all other birds that are native to, or originally from, North America.

The Perfect Stand-In

The turkey vulture has also played an important part in saving a relative from extinction. The California condor once lived all along the West Coast, as far north as Canada and as far south as Baja California in Mexico. By the early 1980s, it survived in only one small, mountainous area of the San Joaquin Valley of California. On the brink of extinction, only a few breeding pairs remained.

Plans were made to place the endangered birds in a captive breeding program at the San Diego Wild Animal Park and the Los Angeles Zoo. In 1987, the last California condor was removed from the wild. So what did the turkey vulture have to do with all this?

Before the condors were taken into captivity, turkey vultures were used as stand-ins to test the cages that were being built and to try out the feeding and other captive-care techniques that would be used for the condors. The turkey vultures, always on the lookout for an easy meal, were willing subjects.

In fact, even after the condors arrived at their "condorminium," as it was called, at the San Diego Wild Animal Park, wild turkey vultures continued to hang around. One clever vulture even managed to break into the new facility. Because the park workers were grateful to learn about this flaw in their system (they didn't want the condors to break out), the vulture was allowed to stay.

Happily, in 1988 the first California condor was hatched in captivity. By 1991, the captive population had nearly doubled, and in 1992, the first young from the program were released into the wild.

Do It Now

Perhaps the condor's story will teach people to protect the earth's wildlife now, whether it is in danger of disappearing or not. Instead of waiting until the last, critical moment, people could work to keep wildlife populations growing when they

Vultures roosting on cacti in a wildlife preserve

decline or keep them stable when they are doing well.

The turkey vulture has managed to hang on over the years and is still relatively common throughout its range. Now is the time to appreciate it for the part it plays in nature and to keep it soaring in the skies.

Sources of Information about Vultures

Write to:

Los Angeles Zoo
5333 Zoo Drive
Los Angeles, CA 90027

Susan Schafer
San Luis Obispo Botanical Garden
P.O. Box 4957
San Luis Obispo, CA 93403

Director
U.S. Fish and Wildlife Service
Department of the Interior
Washington, DC 20240

World Wildlife Fund
Public Information Office
1250 24th Street NW
Washington, DC 20037

Zoological Society of San Diego
P.O. Box 551
San Diego, CA 92112

Call your local museum or zoo to find the name of a bird club or society near you.

Visit your local library and look for these books about vultures and other birds:

Brooks, Bruce. 1989. *On the Wing: The Life of Birds—From Feathers to Flight*. New York: Charles Scribner's Sons.

Cross, Diana Harding. 1981. *Some Birds Have Funny Names*. New York: Crown Publications.

Freschet, Berniece. 1976. *Biography of a Buzzard*. New York: Putnam Publications.

Hume, Rob. 1993. *Birdwatching*. New York: Random House.

MacPherson, Mary. 1988. *Birdwatch: A Young Person's Introduction to Birding*. Toronto: Summerhill Press.

Whitfield, Philip, ed. 1988. *The Macmillan Illustrated Encyclopedia of Birds: A Visual Who's Who in the World of Birds*. New York, Macmillan.

Glossary

adaptation—an adjustment or change to new conditions or surroundings. A plant or animal changes so that it can live in a particular environment.

bird of prey—a bird, such as a hawk, falcon, or vulture, that feeds on carrion (dead animals) or kills other animals for food

breed—to mate and give birth to young

carcass—the body of a dead animal

class—a major group of living things that are alike in certain ways

classify—to arrange living things into groups according to their relationships. One system of classification places all living things into five groups, called kingdoms: plants, animals, monera (bacteria and blue-green algae), fungi, and protists (one-celled living things). Each kingdom is divided into groups. Each group is smaller than the previous group: phylum, class, order, family, genus, and species.

connoisseur (kah-ni-SOOR)—an expert with knowledge and good judgment about art or other topic

down—the soft, fluffy feathers that cover a young bird

endangered—in danger of becoming extinct, or dying out

evolve (ih-VOLV)—to change gradually over a long period of time

fossil—the hardened remains of plants or animals that lived many years ago

habitat (HAB-ih-tat)—the place where an animal or plant naturally lives and grows

hatchling—an animal that has recently come out of its shell

incubate (INK-yuh-bayt)—to hatch eggs by keeping them warm

migrate—to move from one region to another when the season changes

olfactory system (ahl-FAK-tuh-ree)—the parts of the nose and brain that work together to provide the sense of smell

perforated—having a hole

predator (PRED-uh-tuhr)—an animal that lives by killing and eating other animals

preen—to clean and smooth the feathers with the beak

prey—an animal hunted for food by another animal

roost—a group of birds gathered together in one place to rest or sleep; a support on which birds rest

scavenger (SKA-ven-jer)—an animal that feeds on carrion, or the carcasses of dead animals

sibling—a sister or a brother

species (SPEE-sheez)—a group of animals or plants that have certain characteristics in common. Lions and tigers are two different species of cats.

tendon—the cord of tough fiber that fastens a muscle to a bone

thecodont (THEE-kuh-dahnt)—a member of an order of reptiles from about 200 million years ago that had their teeth in sockets and two pairs of openings in the temples of their skulls; they are believed to be ancestors of dinosaurs, birds, and crocodiles

tropical—of the region of the earth along the equator that is noted for its hot, wet climate

vertebrate (VUHR-te-brayt)—an animal that has a spinal column, or backbone. Human beings and other mammals, fish, amphibians, reptiles, and birds have backbones.

Index

About the Author

At her ranch near San Luis Obispo, California, Susan Schafer watches the turkey vultures soaring over the trees in ever-turning, graceful spirals. A freelance writer, Ms. Schafer enjoys sharing her knowledge and appreciation of wildlife and nature with others. For many years she worked at the San Diego Zoo, most recently as curator of reptiles and amphibians.

Ms. Schafer is the author of *The Komodo Dragon* and *The Gálapagos Tortoise*, two other books in the Dillon Remarkable Animals series. Her book on the Gálapagos tortoise was chosen as an Outstanding Science Trade Book for Children in 1992 by the National Science Teachers Association and the Children's Book Council. Ms. Schafer lives in Santa Margarita, California, with her husband, a menagerie of pets, and the wildlife of the oak and pine-studded hills of her backyard.